the BeST FRiENDS book

By Sharon McCoy

Illustrated by Susan Edge
Additional illustrations by Charlene Olexiewicz

A ••fresh•• BOOK

Lowell 🏠 House
Juvenile
Los Angeles

CONTEMPORARY BOOKS
Chicago

To my sisters, Susan Garcia and Shelly Freesemann,
whose best friendships I will treasure forever,
and to Martha Gibson, who has proven over and over again
that water can be as thick as blood

—S.M.

Fresh is an imprint of Lowell House Juvenile, a division of RGA Publishing Group, Inc.

Publisher: Jack Artenstein
General Manager, Juvenile Publishing: Elizabeth D. Wood
Editorial Director: Brenda Pope-Ostrow
Senior Editor: Amy Downing
Cover Design: Lisa-Theresa Lenthall
Interior Design: Michele Lanci-Altomare/Lisa-Theresa Lenthall

Printed in the United States of America

ISBN:1-56565-711-X
Library of Congress Catalog Card Number: 94-35076
10 9 8 7 6 5 4 3 2

CONTENTS

INTRODUCTION

A friend is a person with whom you dare to be yourself.

—AUTHOR UNKNOWN

Who is the one person you can always turn to when things go wrong? Who cheers you up when you feel down? Who can turn a humdrum day into something really spectacular? The one with whom you can laugh, cry, and share your deepest secrets? Your best friend, of course! This book celebrates all those best-friend relationships that make life so special and fun!

Packed inside these pages you'll find loads of useful hints, quizzes, quotes, fill-ins, and tips for you and your friends—all on friendship. You'll learn what being a best friend is all about, and you may even discover things about yourself that you never knew! You'll find great gifts and crafts to make for your friends, no matter what the occasion. And, if you and your pals have ever been bored on a rainy day, you'll never have to wonder what to do again! This book is chock-full of exciting and different activities to do together, regardless if you live next door to your friend or in the next state.

Whether you choose to read the book from cover to cover, or simply flip through the chapters to find the sections you want to devour first, *The Best Friends Book* is sure to help you keep your old friends, make new friends, and even become better friends with the most important person of all—yourself!

1

WHAT FRIENDSHIP IS ALL ABOUT

Finding friends is easy. Keeping them is more difficult.

—AUTHOR UNKNOWN

A best friendship can be one of the most rewarding experiences a girl ever has, but it takes loyalty, honesty, and a real commitment by both you and your pal to make a good friendship work. In this chapter, you and your buddies will find helpful hints and tips for strengthening your friendships and making them better than ever.

BE A BETTER BUDDY

Are you the best friend you can be? Take the quick quiz on the following page and find out. All you have to do is grab a sheet of paper and write down the numbers 1 through 10. Read each question, then put a "T" if the statement is true or an "F" if it's false beside the appropriate number on your paper.

1. I always keep my best friend's secrets.

2. My best friend isn't perfect, but that doesn't change how much I care about her.

3. I never break special plans with my best friend, even if I was invited at the last minute to a supercool party.

4. I can argue with my best friend and not hold grudges.

5. I give my best friend advice without lecturing to her.

6. No matter what we're doing, I always have fun with my best friend.

7. My best friend and I get along great because we can be ourselves around each other.

8. I respect my best friend's interests and opinions, even though I don't share them all.

9. I never try to take away the spotlight from my best friend when it's her turn to shine.

10. I never, ever gossip about my best friend behind her back.

Now, give yourself one point for every answer you marked true. Figure out your "super friend" status using the rating system below. 8–10 points: You're a true-blue pal, and your best friend is lucky to have you in her life! • 5–7 points: You could be a bit more sensitive, but you have the potential. • 1–4 points: Yikes! It's time for you to learn about being a friend. Read on!

TERRIFIC TRAITS

You've heard it before: To *have* a friend, you must *be* a friend. But what does that really mean? For starters, it means putting the Golden Rule into practice and treating others the way you would like to be treated.

Here are the traits every good friend has or should try to have:

- Be a good listener.
- Be accepting.
- Be encouraging.
- Be completely honest.

If you fit all of the above, you're bound to attract quality friendships that will last a lifetime.

ON BEING YOURSELF

There's only one you, and that's what makes you special! You may have all the traits of a perfect friend, but when you try to act like someone you're not, you won't feel good about yourself. What's worse, you'll probably attract friends who aren't right for you, or with whom you have nothing in common.

When you're with your best friend, you know you don't have to pretend to be anyone else—you can just be yourself. Best friends should be able to watch each other cry uncontrollably, laugh hysterically, and act incredibly silly. Once you develop a strong friendship with someone special, that relationship can work like magic to help reinforce who you are and what kind of a person you truly want to be. So, pick your friends carefully and keep in mind that a best buddy should be able to:

- Listen to your fears and insecurities without snickering.
- Give you a shoulder to cry on.
- Keep all your secrets safe.
- Recognize and compliment you on your good qualities.
- Give advice when needed, *without* criticizing.
- Accept you for who you are.

Famous Friendships from Movies

It's Saturday night. Your best friends are coming over for a slumber party. Why not have a movie marathon that really matters? Show your favorite films that feature great friendships! Here are some of the best.

E.T. and Elliot (Henry Thomas) in *E.T.,* 1982

C. C. Bloom (Bette Midler) and Hilary Whitney (Barbara Hershey) in *Beaches,* 1988

M'Lynn (Sally Field), Truvy (Dolly Parton), Ouiser (Shirley MacLaine), Annelle Cici (Daryl Hannah), Claree (Olympia Dukakis), and Shelby (Julia Roberts) in *Steel Magnolias,* 1989

Ariel and Flounder in *The Little Mermaid,* 1989

Vada (Anna Chlumsky) and Thomas James (Macaulay Culkin) in *My Girl,* 1991

Wayne (Mike Myers) and Garth (Dana Carvey) in *Wayne's World,* 1992

Huck Finn (Elijah Wood) and Jim (Robbie Coltrane) in *The Adventures of Huckleberry Finn,* 1993

Mary (Kate Maberly), Colin (Heydon Prowse), and Dickon (Andrew Knott) in *The Secret Garden,* 1993

Jesse (Jason James Richter) and Willy in *Free Willy,* 1993

9

Four Surefire Ways to Foster a Friendship

Ever wonder how some girls get to be *so* popular and have tons of pals, including several best friends? It all starts with liking and respecting yourself. Here are some hints for developing a dynamic duo!

1. *Accept compliments with grace.* If someone pays you a compliment, do you shake your head and say, "Get real!"? If so, you're insulting that person's viewpoint, and at the same time, you're saying that you're not worthy of praise. It's perfectly acceptable, and good for your self-esteem, to smile with appreciation and say, "Thank you!"

2. *Think positive.* Don't put up with putting yourself down. Telling yourself, "Why would *he* ever like me?" or calling yourself a klutz or a space cadet not only makes you feel bad but also sends a terrible message to your friends. Your pals may get tired of repeatedly telling you you're okay and listening to your self-doubts. Start thinking about all the great things you've got going for you!

3. *Trust your own feelings and thoughts.* Do you look to others to either confirm your own opinions or give you direction about how you should think? If so, you're giving the message that you're not confident in your own beliefs. Learn to believe in yourself.

4. Don't blame yourself. When a friend is in a bad mood, do you find yourself thinking, "What did I do wrong? Why is she mad at me?" If you're sure you've done nothing to upset her, don't be so quick to blame yourself. Your energy would be better spent trying to figure out a way to cheer her up!

LONG-DISTANCE FRIENDSHIPS

You've got the greatest best friend in the world, and one day she tells you she's moving away. What should you do?

a) Hire terrorists to hijack the moving truck to Alaska.

b) Pack yourself in a box and move with her.

c) Dry your eyes and read the following tips on keeping faraway friendships going.

Letter c, of course! Grab a hanky and read on!

> "I feel all the same things when I do things alone as when my friend Ole Golly was here. The bath feels hot, the bed feels soft, but I feel there's a funny little hole in me that wasn't there before, like a splinter in your finger, but this is somewhere above my stomach."
> —LOUISE FITZHUGH, HARRIET THE SPY

Games Girls Play

Whether your best friend lives two thousand miles away or just across town, spice up the connection between you and your pal by sending her some creative correspondence!

The Puzzle Letter: Write your friend a one-page letter on plain white paper. (Be sure to include lots of exciting information and juicy news!) When you're done writing, glue the letter to a sheet of cardboard that's the same size as your paper. Wait two hours for the glue to dry, then cut the cardboard into tiny puzzle pieces. Put all the puzzle pieces into a small box and ship it to your pal with T.L.C. (that's Tender Loving Care). She'll have a blast figuring out the mangled message!

Mystery Mail: On a sheet of plain white or colored paper, write your friend a cryptic message using a personalized secret code. Create a symbol for every letter of the alphabet and use the symbols to state your message. For instance, " ❤ ✪❤✳✳ ✳✈☆ " can translate into "I miss you." Be sure to include a copy of the code key so that she can decipher the special saying.

Group Greeting: Take a snapshot of yourself with some of your mutual friends. Tape it to a sheet of sturdy paper and have the whole group write special notes to your buddy and sign their names. Your long-distance friend will be touched beyond belief!

Crossword Connection: Here's a witty way to reminisce. Create a crossword puzzle using special moments or favorite memories as your clues. (For instance: 1 Down—Our favorite food to pig out on; 4 Across—The place we love to spend time.) Refer to the crossword puzzle in the newspaper if you need an example.

Faraway Friend Testimonials

If you or your friend has moved away, whether it's across the country or to the other side of town, you don't have to call it quits. A friendship that flourishes across the miles can be a rewarding and long-lasting union.

The most important aspect of maintaining your friendship is to keep in touch. Before you or she leaves town, agree upon a correspondence schedule. Maybe you can call or write to her every other Saturday, and she can call or write to you twice a month, too.

Listen to what some girls have to say about their long-distance friendships:

I was crushed when Lisa told me her dad got transferred out of state. I thought I'd never be able to smile again! But boy, was I wrong. We're closer than ever before because we write letters and call every week. This summer, my parents are even letting me visit her for two weeks! —Kelsey, 12

Brittany and I met in the fifth grade and she moved away a year later. We've been best friends for three years now. Sure, I've made other friends, but my connection with her is special in spite of the distance. I pour my deepest secrets out to her in letters. Sometimes that's easier than talking face to face! —Ginny, 13

Whenever I'm feeling bummed out or sad, I write a long letter to my best friend in Michigan. She always writes me back and says just the right thing. We'll be best buddies forever . . . I just know it. —Marie, 10

BEST FRIENDS WITH A ... BOY?

Why would a girl want to be best friends with a boy? Probably because he can give her a whole different view on all kinds of situations. And some girls just feel more comfortable hanging around guys than girls.

> **"He is not my boyfriend! He's my friend, and I only surround myself with people I find intellectually stimulating!"**
> —VADA (ANNA CHLUMSKY), FROM THE FILM *MY GIRL*

If you want to strengthen the friendship between you and a guy, or if you already have a boy buddy, here are a few tips:

1. Be prepared to gain a new perspective. Unless you've been hanging around boys all your life, you're probably not accustomed to their ways! Your friend may be able to introduce you to new sports, games, places, and ideas.

Don't turn your nose up at his suggestions before you try them. Then, in return, he may be more willing to join you in your favorite pastimes.

2. Don't feel compelled to explain to the whole world that the two of you are "only friends." In time, others will see that your relationship is based on friendship and nothing else. By making an issue out of it, you may be creating a problem where one doesn't exist.

3. Ask his advice and give some, too! It can be educational and interesting to learn how a boy thinks, and he'll probably be honored that you trust him enough to ask for his opinions. And you can help him out, too, by offering your own ideas and suggestions.

4. Follow the same rules in your boy/girl friendships that you do in your other friendships. Listen to him, and be accepting, encouraging, and honest.

Remember, to have a friend, you must be a friend, even when she's a *he!*

WHEN THREE'S COMPANY

What if your perfect pal pair becomes a tremendous trio? A three-way best friendship can be very rewarding because you have *two* special people to turn to for support and good times. Usually the biggest problem in this type of friendship is that one friend can feel left out and betrayed when the other two go off on their own. If you've got a three-way connection that needs a little extra-special treatment, here are a few awesome activities to do together that will help get things back on track:

1. Have a treasure hunt. One person puts together a series of clues for her two best friends that leads them on a hunt around the neighborhood. When the two "hunters" reach their last clue, the first person will have in mind a special prize, such as treating them to ice cream sundaes or a movie.

2. Go on a picnic. Do a potluck and have each person responsible for a portion of the meal.

3. Put on a play. Two people can be the actors, and the third can be the director and video camera operator. Or, all three friends can make up a skit to perform for family, other buddies, or just a few cherished stuffed animals!

4. Have a study session. If two heads are better than one, then three heads must be the best! (And study breaks are triple the fun!)

Look in chapter 4 for loads of other entertaining activities, regardless of the number of friends involved—a pair, a quartet, or a baker's dozen!

2

RESOLVING PAL PROBLEMS

Real friends are those who, when you've made a fool of yourself,
don't feel that you've done a permanent job.

—AUTHOR UNKNOWN

You feel so lucky! You know you have the best friend anyone could ever ask for. She's your playmate, confidante, ally, and study buddy. She's always there to help when you're in a sticky situation. She laughs at your dumb jokes and tells you you're great even when you don't feel you are. She even puts up with you when you're being a brat! So what happens when a real conflict leaves you both hot under the collar? Do you pack your bags and walk away, or hang tough and try to work through the problem?

66 *The quickest way to spoil a friendship is to wake somebody up in the morning before he is ready!* 99
—E. B. WHITE, CHARLOTTE'S WEB

FIGHTING FAIR WITH YOUR BEST FRIEND

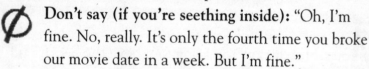

Let's face it. The two of you won't always agree on everything all the time. If you haven't already had a war with your best friend, you can probably count on one happening sometime in the future. And that's okay! It's human nature to disagree, and in the end, you may even strengthen your friendship. Here's what to do when quarrels erupt:

1. Tell her what she did that upset you. If you're angry because she bailed out on a movie date at the very last minute, let her know. Don't keep it inside.

> **Don't say (if you're seething inside):** "Oh, I'm fine. No, really. It's only the fourth time you broke our movie date in a week. But I'm fine."

> **Say:** "I can't believe you broke our movie date! I was counting on seeing that show with you. What happened?"

2. Focus on the actions of your friend rather than your friend, personally. Be clear about the fact that you're unhappy with her behavior and not her as a person. Instead of criticizing her and calling her names, concentrate on how her actions made you feel.

> **Don't say:** "I can't believe how irresponsible you are . . . not to mention inconsiderate and mean. You know how much I wanted to see that movie!"

> **Say:** "When you broke that movie date, it hurt my feelings."

3. Focus your feelings on specifics rather than making generalizations. Using superlatives such as "always" and "never" will only put her on the defensive and she'll be tempted to argue with you.

 Don't say: "You know, you're *always* blowing me off! You *never* follow through with our plans."

 Say: "I was really bummed that you didn't keep your commitment this time."

4. Let her know how her actions made you feel, but don't judge her motives. When you discuss the event that has you upset, don't try and figure out the underlying reason why she hurt you. If you do, she'll probably be so busy defending herself that you'll never resolve the conflict.

 Don't say: "I know you did this on purpose just because you thought I wouldn't get mad. You're always dumping on me!"

 Say: "That movie date was really important to me! Weren't you looking forward to it, too?"

5. Put your energies toward fixing the friendship rather than "winning" an argument. The goal of the argument should be resolving conflict and maintaining your best friendship. Don't try to "win" the fight by offering low blows or criticisms. Focus on reaching a mutual understanding so that you don't get hurt in the same way again.

 Don't say: "Everybody is getting mad at you because you're so unreliable. You're lucky I'm your friend!"

 Say: "I really want us to stay close, but we've got to set some ground rules so that I don't keep getting hurt."

WHEN A FRIEND BETRAYS YOU

A best friend may betray you so badly that you simply can't (or won't) forgive her, even over a period of weeks. Maybe she spread a hurtful rumor about you. Or she told all of your classmates a secret that you had made her *promise* not to tell to anyone. Only you can weigh all of the facts and decide for yourself if you're willing to continue the friendship.

But before you write her off completely, you may want to examine your own best-friend behavior. Did you do something to trigger her betrayal? Perhaps the only way to know for sure is to have a heart-to-heart discussion with her. Also, consider how you'd feel if you lost her as a friend. Do you still value her friendship enough to forgive her for what she did? If so, talk to her right away. Together, come up with a few ways to keep your friendship intact.

> **"The only safe and sure way to destroy an enemy is to make him your friend."**
> —Anonymous

If you feel there's no way to resolve the conflict right now, you still need to take action. Talk to your friend and let her know exactly how you feel. Explain why you're hurt and why you feel the need to back off from the friendship. Then, take some time out and spend several days or even weeks apart. During this time, you should look closely at how you and your friend treat each other.

This separation can be healthy for both of you, since the time apart will allow you to think about what happened and consider how important your friendship is. Problems crop up in almost every friendship. Therefore, the goal is *not* to have any friction between you, but rather to handle it correctly when it occurs!

4 Quick and Easy Ways to Turn an Enemy into a Friend

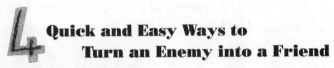

Use one or several of the tips below to turn a foe into a friend!

1. Make peace. Take the first step toward a truce by offering your apologies. Be willing to admit, "I was wrong and I'm sorry."

2. Forgive your foe. You can't move forward and become friends until you forgive your enemy—but you have to mean it!

3. Honor her with honesty. Practice being completely truthful with your feelings. If you lie to her, you are saying either that you don't care enough about her to be truthful, or that you don't trust the friendship enough to confide in her.

4. Kill her with kindness. Do something sweet and sincere for your adversary and she won't stay mad for long!

WHEN YOUR PARENTS DON'T LIKE YOUR BEST BUDDY

You're supertight with your best friend, but your parents think she's the female equivalent of Bart Simpson! Take steps to smooth out the situation. Below are some useful guidelines for making peace between your parents and your pal.

- Find out why your parents don't approve of your friend. Listen with an open mind and try not to get angry. Perhaps they know something about your friend that you don't. Chances are, your parents are just concerned for your welfare, and for some reason they believe your best friend isn't a positive influence on you.

- If you sincerely believe that your friend is worth keeping and that she's good for you, write a letter to your parents explaining all the things you like about your friend. This act is bound to impress them.

- Show your parents that you are a responsible person and that you and your pal do *not* imitate Beavis and Butt-head when you're together! Your mature behavior might prove to your parents that no one will *cause* you to get into trouble. Once your folks see your maturity, they'll begin trusting you to pick your own friends.

- Plan an activity that you, your friend, and your parents can do together. The more time you and your friend spend with Mom and Dad, the more they'll see your pal's prized qualities.

How to Make (and Keep!) a Best Friend

Ask yourself, "Would I like to be best friends with me right now?" The following exercises can help make sure that you're on the right track!

- Write down your personality traits, both good and bad. Ask yourself: Do people generally like me? Why or why not? Take pride in all the great things that make you you, and work on those qualities that need a little improvement.

- Listen in on your own conversations. Do you let your friends speak freely, or do you interrupt and give too much advice where it's not wanted?

- Try to learn what makes your friends tick. Use your natural curiosity to find out more about them and what they like and don't like. When a friend is talking, listen attentively. If you're genuinely interested in her, she'll be interested in you, too!

- Give your friends a chance to shine. If a friend is telling a funny joke to a crowd and enjoying the attention, don't chime in with the punch line. No one wants to be overshadowed by their friends!

- Don't gossip or agree with someone who loves flapping her lips about everyone and everything! If you don't feel like defending the person who is being talked about, simply state that you feel uncomfortable with the subject and walk away.

If you treat others as you would like to be treated, you will never have to worry about whether your friends really like you. Your biggest problem will be finding enough time to spend with all your best friends!

FIX THOSE FRIENDSHIPS!

Now it's time to visit the neighborhood Friend Improvement shop with Evvyone Kneeds Help. (Her friends call her Ms. Evvy.) She knows the ins and outs of friendships, because she's constantly working to make them better!

New Kid on the Block

Q Dear Ms. Evvy: I just moved to another state and I'm miserable! I've always gone to school with the same kids. I was popular, had lots of friends, and was a good student. I want to make friends here, but I don't know how. Help!

L.H., San Diego, California

A Starting over at a new school can be a major challenge. But since you were well liked at your old school, had many friends, and made good grades, there's no reason that you won't be accepted in your new school, too. All the qualities that made you a valued member of your old circle are the same ones that will help you now. Give yourself lots of opportunities to mix and mingle with different groups of people . . . and don't forget to smile!

Put Down and Put Off

Q Dear Ms. Evvy: My best friend has been ganging up with another friend and putting me down. When I complain, they say, "We were just kidding," or "Don't be so sensitive." I'm sick of taking their criticisms. What should I do?

A.P., *Winona, Minnesota*

 Your pals aren't playing fair! When you defend yourself, they put the blame back on you by saying you're too sensitive. Get out of the hurtful trap you're in. Start to involve yourself in activities with other people. Chances are, you'll make some new friends—ones that won't feel the need to put you down. And once your best friend sees that you won't stand for her ill treatment of you, she may stop dishing the dirt!

> "A false friend and a shadow attend only when the sun shines."
> —BEN FRANKLIN, INVENTOR AND PHILOSOPHER

Too Much of a Good Thing

Dear Ms. Evvy: I'm kind of known as the person everyone can trust and count on. My best friend is always telling me her problems and asking for advice. Even though I love to listen and help, I'm so busy figuring out her life that I don't have time for mine! What should I do?

L.C., *Idaho Falls, Idaho*

Your role as listener and advice-giver is certainly an admirable one, but as you've discovered, it can be a burden. Start by approaching your friend with a problem of your own. She'll probably be glad that she can help you out in return. After all, friendship is a two-way street.

The Truth Counts

Q Dear Ms. Evvy: My best friend told me she got an A on a paper right after I showed her that I got an A. Then, the assignment fell out of her notebook and I saw a huge red C written on it. Why would she lie to me about something so trivial? It makes me wonder if she lies about big things, too.

T.H., Loveland, Colorado

A There could be many reasons why your friend fibbed about her grade, but most likely she was embarrassed about the C. Perhaps the grade seemed trivial to you, but if she has a difficult time in school, she may feel threatened by you and other students. The important thing now is to talk about the incident. Let her know that you'll accept her and be her best friend no matter what grade she gets. Explain how important honesty is to you. Don't assume that she's been dishonest in the past, either.

Flawed Friendship

Q Dear Ms. Evvy: My best friend of five years just transferred to a private school. Lately, she's become snotty and very distant. She even told me that I needed to go on a diet and that my hair looked terrible! She's always saying how popular she is at her new school and how everyone likes her. I feel bad whenever we're together. What can I do?

W.V., Portland, Oregon

A Perhaps your friend is actually feeling insecure with her new surroundings and is bragging to you in order to build up her ego. Maybe she's made the mistake of believing that by putting you down, she'll build herself up. That doesn't mean that you have to stand for it. Friends are supposed to make you feel better about yourself, not worse. Let her know that her behavior is making you feel awful, and unless she makes a quick turnaround, you're not going to hang around her for a while. She'll either change back to her former self, or leave you free to enjoy new friends who will give you positive reinforcement.

> **"**Like it or not, we've got to be together on this raft for a long time," said the king to the duke. "What's the use of you being so sour? . . . Let's shake hands and be friends.**"**
>
> —MARK TWAIN, THE ADVENTURES OF HUCKLEBERRY FINN

A History of Famous TV Friendships

In TV land, friendships are built, destroyed, then put back together again—all in a thirty-minute time slot. Here are some of the best TV-made friendships in television history, many of which you can catch either on prime time or a syndicated station.

Blossom (Mayim Bialik) and Six (Jenna Von Oy) in "Blossom"

Lois (Teri Hatcher) and Clark (Dean Cain) in "Lois & Clark: The New Adventures of Superman"

Tia (Tia Mowry) and Tamara (Tamara Mowry) in "Sister, Sister"

Lucy (Lucille Ball) and Ethel (Vivian Vance) in "I Love Lucy"

Mary (Mary Tyler Moore) and Rhoda (Valerie Harper) in "The Mary Tyler Moore Show"

Laverne (Penny Marshall) and Shirley (Cindy Williams) in "Laverne & Shirley"

Kelly (Jennie Garth) and Donna (Tori Spelling) in "Beverly Hills, 90210"

3

GIFTS AND CRAFTS FOR 4-EVER FRIENDS

This is my advice. Give one glittering scale
(your most prized possession) to each of the other fish.
You will no longer be the most beautiful fish in the sea,
but by giving of yourself you'll discover how to be happy.

—MARCUS PFISTER, THE RAINBOW FISH

Your friend spends a whole weekend helping you with your chores, and then she listens to you sob for hours over not making the school's soccer team. Or, maybe the two of you have just made up after experiencing World War III. What can you do to show that you care? Let her know how important she is to you with creative and memorable gifts you make yourself.

> **"A friend is a present which you give yourself."**
> —ROBERT LOUIS STEVENSON, AUTHOR

THE BIRTHDAY TREE

You don't need a green thumb to give this friendship plant—just a little thoughtfulness and some imagination!

You need:

- small tree or large plant
- wrapping paper, ribbon
- friendship mementos (pictures, ticket stubs, etc.)

What to do:

1. About a week before your friend's birthday, go to the nursery or garden center and look at the miniature trees (the kind that grow in pots) or the flowering plants. Buy an especially beautiful one that is blooming or just about to bloom. Be sure to get the nursery to write down the care and watering instructions so you can include them with your gift.

2. To give your gift some birthday flair, tape colorful wrapping paper around the pot and add a cute bow. Hang a card from one of the limbs. You can hang other mementos as well, such as old snapshots, secret notes, and dried flowers.

3. When you present your friend with the special gift, don't forget to point out to her that the tree will bloom right around her birthday every year!

10 Reasons to Give a Gift to a Friend

1. To say thanks: She helped you study for a big test and you both aced it.

2. To help her through a change: She's just moved into a new house or she just found out she has to share her bedroom with her sister.

3. To celebrate a fun event: The two of you just had a great time together, such as enjoying a concert, a bike ride, or a special trip.

4. Because you remember: While shopping one day, you noticed how much she admired something, so you took the time to buy or make it for her.

5. To celebrate a job well done: Did she make the school volleyball team or was she just elected president of her class?

6. To cheer her up: Everybody has a bad day now and then. A small gift from a special best friend can really brighten up her day.

7. Pass it on: You have a sweater or other item that you don't like but she has always loved. Give it to her, as long as it's okay with Mom or Dad.

8. Double dilemma: If you receive a gift of something you already have, give the duplicate to your friend.

9. To say you're sorry: Maybe it wasn't even a fight, but there was a misunderstanding. Besides apologizing, a small gift can go a long way toward patching things up again.

10. Just because: No special reason—you just wanted to give your friend a gift she'll never forget.

DOUBLE THE FUN EARRINGS

Are you short on time, but you want the world to know you're best friends? This is a gift you'll love as much as the lucky recipient!

You need:

- small box
- pretty ribbon
- 2 pairs of inexpensive earrings that look good together

What to do:

1. Go shopping for two pairs of inexpensive earrings that complement each other, such as two different colored pairs that represent your school colors, or a pair of earrings in her favorite color and a pair in your favorite color. You can even mix ideas. If she likes dogs and you like cats, find one pair of earrings with dogs and another pair with cats.

2. Now, do a switcheroo! Put one earring from one set and one earring from the other set into a small box. Wrap it up with a ribbon.

3. Give it to your best friend with a note. You keep the other earrings! Now you and your friend can wear your pairs of earrings together to show everyone you two are a perfect match.

Famous Friendship Songs

Do you have a friend who's been feeling a little down? Pop one of these tunes into your CD player or request one on your favorite radio station and dedicate it to your blue buddy—then watch her blues float away!

"Whenever I Call You Friend,"
Kenny Loggins

"You've Got a Friend,"
James Taylor

"That's What Friends Are For,"
Dionne Warwick

"You're My Best Friend,"
Queen

"Me and My Friends,"
Red Hot Chili Peppers

"Anytime You Need a Friend,"
Mariah Carey

"Find Yourself a Friend,"
Hammer

"I Could Have Been Your Best Friend," Bonnie Raitt

"He's My Best Friend,"
Jellyfish

"I Will Be Your Friend,"
Sade

"If You Really Want to Be My Friend," Rolling Stones

FRIENDSHIP PHOTO CALENDAR

You've been best friends as long as you can remember, and you want to give her a gift that will last all year. Whip up a whole year of wonderful memories that your friend can enjoy for 365 days and then treasure as a keepsake for years to come.

You need:

- inexpensive month-by-month calendar, with an image above each month
- white glue
- scissors
- photos of you and your best friend taken throughout the year
- 12 sheets of construction paper, various colors
- old magazines and newspapers
- wax paper
- colored pens

What to do:

1. Gather memorabilia that represents your special friendship, such as pictures, ticket stubs, napkins, flowers, or even cutouts from magazines of the types of things your best friend loves to do.

2. Separate these things into twelve piles to represent the months of the year. You may want to give each month a different theme, such as memorabilia of summer activities in July, preparing for school in August, and colorful fall pictures in September.

3. Open the calendar so that the month of January shows. Lay the pictures and cutouts you've designated for January over the calendar photograph, overlapping them until the calendar image is completely covered. If there are any open

spaces, simply cover them up with small pieces of colored construction paper. Now glue these cutouts into place. As you create each collage, place a piece of wax paper on top of it. Then, as you turn the calendar pages, they will stay separated, and if any glue seeps out, your pages won't stick together. Leave the wax paper in place overnight to dry.

4. When the glue has dried, remove the wax paper. Go through the calendar and mark off special days such as her birthday, friends' birthdays, the first and last days of school, holidays, and the best concerts coming to town.

5. Finally, decorate the front and back covers of the calendar. You may want to take a special photograph of you and your best friend together. Have a family member take one picture of the two of you facing the camera for the front cover, and a second shot of you and your friend with your backs to the camera for the back of the calendar. Don't tell your friend what the pictures are for. Then, when she receives her personalized calendar, she'll be touched beyond belief!

> ❝You give but little when you give of your possessions. It is when you give of yourself that you truly give.❞
> —KAHLIL GIBRAN, AUTHOR AND ARTIST

THREE QUICK 'N' THOUGHTFUL GIFTS FOR A FRIEND

Giving really is better than receiving, especially when you see how much your friend loves these cool homemade gifts that don't cost a lot, but still show how much you're thinking of her.

1. Pen Pick-Me-Up

If your friend just finished a big brain-draining test, whether she aced it or bombed it, buy her a felt-tip marker in her favorite color. Glue a picture of her favorite cartoon character's head to the end of the pen that sticks up when you're writing. Include a note with the pen that says, "Congrats, girl!" or "Better luck next time!" This thoughtful, silly gift is sure to put a smile on her face.

2. The Lovin' Oven

Buy a roll of packaged sugar cookie dough from the refrigerator section of the supermarket. Roll out the dough.

With a simple gingerbread cookie cutter, cut cookies out in the shape of gingerbread girls. Bake them, then decorate them to look like your best friend and other classmates. "Dress" the cookies with icing, colored to imitate the latest fashions.

3. Tantalizing Tees

Got a friend who's down in the dumps? Give her something to get her back in the groove with a special T-shirt made just for her. Buy a T-shirt, then grab a couple of fabric markers in your friend's favorite colors and begin writing down all the words that best describe her. Is she athletic . . . brainy . . . cool . . . crafty . . . clever . . . cute . . . dramatic . . . funny? This gift should help to make her day.

THE KEY TO GIFT GIVING

When you give something to a friend, make it an offering from your heart. Don't ever feel you must buy somebody's friendship in order to be accepted. Spending a lot of money will only drain your pocketbook.

The time and effort you put into thinking, planning, and creating a personal present will be appreciated more than the gift itself, and it will express the real depth and meaning of your friendship. A handmade gift says to your friend and to the world, "My best friend is one very special person!"

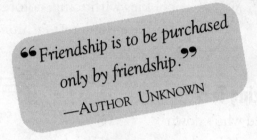

Friendship is to be purchased only by friendship.
—AUTHOR UNKNOWN

THINGS TO DO WITH YOU-KNOW-WHO!

The most I can do for my friend is simply to be his friend.

—HENRY DAVID THOREAU, AUTHOR

O ne of the best ways to develop strong friendships is through spending time together. Of course, sitting around watching old reruns of "Gilligan's Island" or "The Brady Bunch" is not the most ideal pastime on which to build a friendship!

This chapter is devoted to fresh, creative activities to give you and your buddies some great ideas for spending time together, while enhancing your friendship at the same time.

THE RAINY DAY RETREAT

Ideal number of friends: two or four (pairs are ideal)
Just because the weather seems to be working against you doesn't mean you and your best friend can't have

a great time. Join the most exclusive of spas—the one in your home or hers—and give yourselves a marvelous makeover with ingredients right from your own kitchen. (The items you need to provide are in bold.)

The evening before:

1. Make sure it's okay with your parents to commandeer your bedroom and one bathroom the next day for several hours.

2. Read through the retreat below and collect all the materials you'll need for your big day.

The retreat!

8 A.M.: With your buddy, start your rainy day retreat by working out to the hottest new **exercise video** your rental store has to offer. Or, if you have a large garage or basement, grab a **jump rope**, turn on your **favorite tunes**, and jump rope for twenty to forty minutes, depending on your level of fitness. Then, do some of your favorite floor exercises (is there such a thing?), like sit-ups or leg-lifts. Stretch out your muscles for at least ten minutes when you are done.

9:30 A.M.: Cool down from your workout with a fresh, healthy fruit smoothie. Place one to two cups of **fresh fruit** (strawberries, bananas, and oranges work well), one cup of **milk**, and one cup of **ice** into a **blender**. Blend on high until smooth. Pour into two **tall glasses** and top with **straws**. (Depending on the number of spa enthusiasts, increase the recipe as needed.)

10 A.M.: Next, take turns taking a steamy shower and washing your hair.

10:30 A.M.: After you've dried off, put on some comfortable sweats and prepare to condition your hair. In a **small bowl**, beat an **egg** with a **fork**. If you have long hair, use two eggs. Rub the beaten egg mixture into your damp hair. Wrap your hair in a **towel** and let the conditioner set for fifteen minutes.

10:45 A.M.: Rinse out the conditioner. Do not use hot water or the egg mixture could turn into scrambled eggs!

11 A.M.: Now you're ready to give each other a facial, or mask, which you can make yourself from one of the recipes following the retreat.

12 NOON: Lunch break! Load up on fresh **veggies** in a big **salad**. Skip the cookies for dessert and eat an **apple** instead.

1 P.M.: Trade off fixing each other's hair. If your damp hair has a case of the tangles, *don't* use a brush. This can snap the ends and cause split ends. Instead, gently use a comb to separate the tangles. Work from the ends of your hair up to your scalp. If one of you has long, straight hair, you can braid the hair while it is still wet. Remove the braids when the hair is dry and you'll have instant waves. If you get stumped for other hairstyling ideas, refer to your favorite fashion **magazines** for inspiration.

2:30 P.M.: Once your hair is perfect, you can give each other a manicure. Begin by soaking your hands in a **small bowl** of warm water and a little **dishwashing soap**. Gently scrub your nails with the **nail brush**, and very gently push back the cuticles. Do not clip or cut them. Lightly shape the nails with an **emery**

board. Pick out a dazzling shade of **nail polish**. While your nails are drying, talk about all the fantastic things you're going to do when the weather clears up.

4 P.M.: What a day! You've pampered yourself all day long and had lots of fun with your friend. Host another retreat the next time you and your buddies want to do something special for yourselves—there's no need to wait for rain!

Cool Make-It-Yourself Masks

Avocado Smoother: The avocado smoother will give any skin a silky, softer appearance.

Mix one-half medium-sized ripe **avocado**, one tablespoon of **honey**, and a quarter cup of **milk** in a **blender** or a **bowl** with a **fork** until smooth. Pin back your hair away from your face. Starting at your neck, gently massage the mixture onto your skin. Work your way up to your face, with upward strokes. Make sure you leave a one-inch area around your eyes to protect them. Sit back, put your feet up, and relax for about twenty minutes.

Splash off the mask with warm water and then rinse with cool water. Your skin and pores will feel great.

Egg Facials: If you prefer egg on your face, try one of these two egg-citingly simple beauty masks.

EGG FACIAL #1: Mix together one fresh **egg** and enough **honey** to make a paste. Spread this mix over your face, leaving a one-inch area around your eyes. Let the mask harden for fifteen to twenty minutes. Rinse with warm water to remove the mask, then splash your face with cool water to soothe your skin and tighten your pores.

EGG FACIAL #2: Have an adult help you separate the **egg whites** from the egg yolk. You will need two egg whites per girl. Beat the whites with a **fork** or an **electric beater** until frothy. Spread the whites over your face and throat, leaving a one-inch area around your eyes. Let the mask dry for fifteen to twenty minutes before rinsing with cold water. The egg whites will close your pores and make your face look clean and shiny.

66 'I am going to Oz to get my brains at last. When I return, I shall be like your other friends with brains,' said Scarecrow.
'I have always liked you as you were,' Dorothy said. 99
—L. FRANK BAUM, THE WIZARD OF OZ

BUSINESS BUDDIES

Ideal number of friends: three to five

If your funds seem to be constantly running on empty, think about teaming up with a few friends and starting a business. Not only can you fatten up your piggy bank, but you're sure to have a blast doing it! The steps below will help you and your friends organize any business ideas you may have. (Some possible businesses are listed on page 46. Pick something that you and your friends all enjoy, or come up with an original, supercreative plan!)

1. Get permission. Before you get too excited about making money, check with your parents. Taking on a part-time job is a big responsibility. Be prepared to show your parents how you will budget your time and still accomplish all of your regular chores and school activities.

2. Plan it. Once you get the thumbs-up sign, hold a planning session with your friends. Each of you should make a list of the things you are good at and enjoy doing. Use the lists to compare your strengths and weaknesses, then try to come up with a job everyone would like to do. Does everyone in the group love children? Then a baby-sitting service is a natural. Or maybe everyone's favorite thing to do is to make arts and crafts. Set up a craft booth or go door-to-door selling handmade gifts.

3. Divide up the responsibilities. Although everyone should pitch in to make the products or perform a particular service, each of you may need to take on an additional responsibility to get the work done most effectively. Below you will find various job titles, each covering an important task. Depending on the size of your business and group of friends, one person may be able to handle two jobs, or you may need two or three people to handle one job!

The advertiser hands out fliers to neighbors and friends and thinks of creative ways to drum up business. This person is also responsible for making the fliers as well as any posters.

The scheduler is responsible for setting up a schedule that works for the workers and the clients (those people who pay for your service or product). If one of the workers is ill or unavailable, this person needs to make sure someone can take her place. Otherwise, the scheduler should call the client to reschedule a time.

The treasurer is in charge of collecting money from the clients and paying the workers. Some of the earnings should be used to buy any supplies as well. If you're decorating T-shirts, you'll have a long supply list, but if you're house-sitting, you may not need to buy any business materials.

4. *Work out the details.* At this time, you need to get your friends together and work out any additional details. These will vary depending on your service or product, but here are some basic things to keep in mind:

- How much will you charge for your service or product? (One of the best ways to set prices is to find out how much the competition charges.)

- What days will you work?

- Do you want a business name?

- Do you need to contact your local chamber of commerce for any licenses or permissions?

5. *Take pride in your work.* When your first offer rolls in, do the very best job you can. The best kind of advertisement is a job well done. Be proud of what you have accomplished. When the job is finished, you and your friends should celebrate together.

Brilliant Business Ideas

Below you will find several job ideas for you and your friends to explore, along with helpful tips on each.

Cleaning: Washing windows, vacuuming, scrubbing bathrooms, and making beds can be profitable. With a friend or two, you'll get a lot more work done in less time.

Baby-sitting: If there's more than one child in the family, baby-sitting with a buddy can help to even the odds and make the time seem to fly by. (Remember, though, your responsibility is taking care of the kids, not each other!)

Yard work: It's probably best to leave heavy mowing to adults with power mowers, but you can still earn money weeding gardens, sweeping driveways, or watering plants.

Vacation service: Let your neighbors know they can go away on vacation and not have to worry about feeding the pet, watering the plants, or bringing in the mail. With you and a friend or two pulling the load together, you can either alternate days and duties or do it as a team.

THE FRIENDSHIP GARDEN

Ideal number of friends: two

Growing a small garden is a great way to cultivate a friendship! You and your friend can choose special flowers to symbolize the memorable things you've shared. Your garden will grow and bloom into a living memento of your friendship. (The items you need to provide are in bold.)

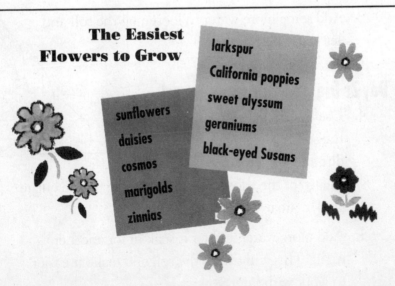

The Easiest Flowers to Grow

larkspur

California poppies

sweet alyssum

geraniums

black-eyed Susans

sunflowers

daisies

cosmos

marigolds

zinnias

Day 1: Plan and prep it!

1. With your parents' okay, pick a **small plot of land** in your backyard, about three feet by four feet, in a sunny location. (If you live in an apartment, an outdoor planter box will work.) Spend a few hours after school or on a weekend getting your garden ready. Wet the area thoroughly with a **hose** to make it easier to dig. Use a **shovel** to dig up any grass or weeds.

2. Then dig a nice, neat trench, three to four inches deep, around the garden area. This will help to keep the weeds and grass from growing back and smothering your flowers.

3. Add some more water to loosen up the soil and let it sit overnight.

Day 2: Dig and dig some more!

4. Use the shovel to turn, or aerate, the soil by digging up clumps of dirt and breaking them up with the tip of the shovel. You need to dig up the entire garden area.

5. Add more water and let it soak in for another night. This will soften the soil and make it easier to work with later.

48

6. Go to a nursery or garden center with your friend to pick up **eight small plants** (two different types of flowers) for your garden. You can always add more flowers later. Make your choices based first on the climate where you live and second on what kind of flowers you like. Planting and watering instructions are available at your garden center.

Day 3: Plant and position it!

7. On the third day you are ready to plant. With your hands, shape the dirt you've dug up into neat rows. You will place the plants into the mounds of dirt. The lower areas between the rows are for water drainage. Plan on using one or two small plants for every square foot of garden space.

8. With the shovel, dig a small hole in a dirt mound you've created, large enough to fit one of your plants. Carefully remove your plant from its container. Try to keep as much dirt around the roots as possible. Keeping the plant in its own dirt will help to prevent it from going into transplant shock. Place the plant into the hole and cover the roots with dirt.

9. Continue until you have planted all the plants. Water lightly with a **watering can**.

Day 4: Enjoy it!

10. Now that your garden is planted, you and your best friend can either take turns watering and weeding or do the tasks together. In a few weeks or months, you will be rewarded with big, beautiful flowers to press, dry, and pick for each other!

Say It with Flowers!

Whether they're for a gift or a garden, here are some special flowers and what they mean.

Apple blossoms mean I prefer you.

Red chrysanthemums mean I love you.

White chrysanthemums mean truth.

White daisies stand for innocence.

Forget-me-nots mean true love.

Gardenias mean secret love.

Ivy signifies friendship.

Jasmine stands for joy.

White lilies mean sweetness.

Petunias stand for soothing.

Red roses mean love.

Pink roses are for simplicity.

Yellow roses are for friendship.

Blue violets are for faithfulness.

Zinnias represent thoughts of absent friends.

ACTIVITIES FOR TEN (OR MORE!)

If you have ten or more friends, you've got an instant party. Here are a few zany ideas to entertain the masses. (The items you need to provide are in bold.)

Pizza Potluck

1. Tell everyone to bring her favorite pizza topping. You supply the **tomato sauce** and **mini-pizza crusts**. Flour tortillas or English muffins work well as pizza crusts.

2. With an adult's help, turn on the **oven broiler**. Arrange the toppings on **plates** or in **bowls** on the counter and let each girl build her own pizza.

3. With an adult's help, put the pizzas on a **cookie sheet** and pop it in the broiler until the cheese is melted and bubbly. When they are ready, have an adult remove the hot pizzas.

4. Sit on the floor, break out a **board game** or the latest **video**, and chow down!

The Bad-Hair-Day Scavenger Hunt

1. Before your guests arrive, prepare a **list of weird and wacky items** that relate to hair for your friends to track down on this scavenger hunt. (See "Scavenger Hunt Hints" on page 52 for ideas.) Make sure you and each team have a copy of the list.

2. When your friends arrive, divide them up into two teams according to the hair theme. Separate the blondes and brunettes, short-haired and long-haired, whatever!

3. Give each team a copy of the list and set a time limit of one hour. Send everyone out into the neighborhood to see how many of the items on the list they can find.

4. When both teams return, check the items off the lists. The team that found the most stuff wins. If both teams found the same number of items, the team who made it back first is the winner. The losing team has to give themselves new hair makeovers, using as many of the scavenger items as possible!

Scavenger Hunt Hints

Use this list or add some ideas of your own. Make them as challenging as possible!

red curly wig

frilly pink hair ribbon

bottle of hair conditioner at least three years old

black comb with dandruff

wig with a purple or blue dyed strand (Hint: Girls can "dye" a hair strand themselves with a purple or blue marker.)

broken curling iron

three different kinds of hair rollers (pink sponge rollers, steam rollers, spiked rollers)

pink hairbrush

rubberband with hair in it

barrette with ribbons attached

stretched-out scrunchee (ponytail holder)

bottle of any temporary hair coloring

any hair accessory your mother might have worn when she was a girl

BONUS: 1 point for each doll brought in, each with a different color of hair!

Water-athalon

If things are heating up, you and your friends can cool off with this wild water workout.

1. Have each girl bring the equipment for one water activity. Here are just a few hot-weather ideas to keep everyone cool:

    -   Have a squirt gun fight.

    -   Split up into teams and throw water balloons.

    -   Use the hose as a jump rope. Each time someone messes up, she gets squirted with the hose.

    -   Have a Bucket Brigade Relay Race. Divide into teams, then race across the yard holding cups of water to see who can be first to fill a bucket.

- Play Marco Polo blindfolded, but instead of calling out "Marco Polo," spray the person who is "it" with a squirt gun.

- Have a dance contest in the sprinklers (to the hottest music, of course).

- Hold a water-spitting contest to see who can spit the farthest.

2. Put on your bathing suits, slap on some **sunscreen**, and go for it!

Far-Out Fashions

With your pals, create original outfits with this fun activity that pushes your fashion sense to the limit!

1. Tell your friends to bring their favorite accessories, such as belts, pins, vests, hats, and suspenders.

2. Divide into teams. Hand each team **five oversized plain T-shirts**, a pair of **scissors**, and some **fabric markers** to create their ultimate fashion statements. No other sewing or craft tools are allowed. They can use all five T-shirts for one outfit or make several outfits from all the shirts. Set a time limit of one hour.

3. When the creations are complete, each team should pick models to show them off. Crank up the **music** and start the fashion parade!

4. Have a **camera** or **video camera** handy to record the results.

Making a Difference

You and your close friends bring out the best in each other. Together, you can also bring out the best in your community.

1. Choose a project or activity in your neighborhood or community that means a lot to you and your friends. Maybe it's a park that needs cleaning, graffiti that needs painting over, a busy street that needs a crosswalk, or a homeless shelter that is in need of supplies.

2. Write a letter to your city or county officials and tell them about the problem. The names and addresses of local authorities can be found in your city's phone directory. The letter should say exactly how you and your friends feel about the situation. Include your name, address, and phone number.

3. All your friends should sign the letter. If the problem affects a large group of people, you and your friends should ask neighbors, teachers, and store owners to sign the letter as well. (You can attach additional sheets of paper to the letter.)

4. Send the signatures along with your letter to the local officials. You may want to send a copy of it to the editor of your city's newspaper as well. The more people you get to see and understand the problem, the more attention you will get from city and county authorities.

A little bit of work can make a big difference to improve where and how you live!

BETTER THAN BUDDY BUILDING

If you and your best friends have worked your way
completely through this chapter, you have had a lot of
fun. You probably know each other better than you ever
thought you would. You've been healthy, earned money,
planted a garden, showed off your "flair for fashion," and
set out to change a part of your world. Most importantly
you've begun forging friendships to last a lifetime.

Don't stop here, though. Come up with your own
ideas for things to do, then do them. Don't be afraid to set
new trends and get a little crazy. Remember, one of the
best things about having good friends is that you can
always be yourself around them!

5

EVERYTHING I EVER WANTED TO KNOW ABOUT MY BEST BUDS

A friend is one who knows all about you and still likes you.

—AUTHOR UNKNOWN

H ow well do you really know your best friend? Learn some things you probably never knew about her, just by fillng out the following fun and handy reference list. Once you get the facts down in black and white, you'll be able to remember superspecial details about your best friend. There is one section here to fill out on one of your most special friends, but you can always add your own pages to gather information on other V.I.P.s (Very Important Pals).

FIRST THINGS FIRST

Your friend's full name:

This is how she signs her name (get her signature here):

_____

I call her:

Address:

Phone number:

Her birthday is:

Birthstone:

Gifts she would flip over:

Gifts you've given her in the past:

This is what she looks like
(put her picture here):

PERSONAL FAVES

Favorite color:

Types of clothing she loves:

Brand of clothing she likes to wear:

Favorite class:

Favorite teacher:

Who she's got a crush on:

Hobby she most enjoys:

Craft she prefers to do:

Sport she likes to play or watch:

Favorite book:

Favorite movie:

Actor she adores:

Actress she'd most like to be:

Song she loves to sing in the shower:

Favorite tape/CD:

Favorite group:

Perfume she wears all the time:

PERSONAL BESTS

At school, she's tops in:

Her best sport is:

She's so talented when it comes to:

Her greatest achievement is:

THINK ON IT!

Get together with your friend and interview her, using the following questions. You'll laugh, learn, and maybe even shed a few sentimental tears!

1. If your friend were magically granted three wishes, what would she wish for?

2. Would she rather be an actress, famous singer, renowned athlete, or President of the United States? Why?

3. If she could change one thing about herself, what would it be?

4. If she were a scientist, what disease would she hope to cure first?

5. What famous woman does she most admire and why?

6. If she could live in another century or decade, what would it be and why?

7. What three places in the world would she visit if she could travel anywhere?

8. If she could adopt any one quality from any well-known person, what would it be and who would it be from?

INSIDER INFO

66 *Friendship is the only cement that will ever hold the world together.* 99
—AUTHOR UNKNOWN

1. What is your most unforgettable memory together?

2. What is your most embarrassing moment together?

3. What were the circumstances (date, time, place, event) when you two met for the first time?

4. What is the biggest secret you share that no one else knows?

5. What is the one thing you're *sure* you'll do together in the years to come?

THE BEST FRIENDS COMPATIBILITY QUIZ

Is your friendship a match made in heaven? Take this compatibility quiz alone or with your best friend. Circle the answers that best describe your relationship.

1. Your and your best friend's favorite thing to do together is:
   a) hang out with a big group of people.
   b) go to a movie.
   c) anything! Neither of you cares what you do as long as you're together!

2. When it comes to conflicts, you and your best friend:
   a) have never had a misunderstanding; you agree with her on everything because you don't want to upset her.
   b) seem to disagree quite a bit.
   c) have occasional arguments, which usually bring you closer together in the end.

3. When you or your best friend says or does something that makes the other one angry, you both:
   a) ignore it—it's not your place to try and change each other.
   b) ask each other not to do it again.
   c) tell each other how the behavior made you feel and work to resolve the conflict.

4. If you or she were celebrating a birthday, you'd be most likely to:
   a) do nothing. You both usually have plans with other people.
   b) call each other and offer birthday wishes.
   c) make plans to spend the special day doing something together.

5. You or your best friend starts hanging out with a new friend, and you now spend less time together. What's your reaction?
   a) Neither of you care—you've both got plenty of other friends.
   b) You both have hurt feelings but don't want to intrude on the other friendship.
   c) You tell each other how hurt you are that you are drifting apart, and you want to do something about it.

6. Your best friend tells you a startling secret about her and someone else you know. You:
   a) tell just one friend—you're sure she won't tell anyone else.
   b) ask your pal if you can repeat the news to someone else.
   c) keep her secret safe—you wouldn't betray her confidence.

7. You and your best friend have totally different opinions on a particular subject. You:
   a) try to sway each other's opinion—she thinks she's right, but you know you're right!
   b) disagree with each other but say nothing.
   c) respect each other's opinion even though you don't share it.

8. You or your best friend is in a rotten mood. You:
   a) avoid each other since there's no reason to make the other one miserable, too.
   b) still hang out together but say nothing about your feelings.
   c) let your emotions out—you both can be totally real around each other.

Now, give yourself two points for every "c" answer, one point for every "b" answer, and zero points for every "a" answer. Total up the numbers, then turn the page to see how your friendship rates!

12–16: FRIENDS 4-EVER! She's an unbeatable buddy! It's you for her and her for you . . . always! You two share common interests and have tons of fun together, and you respect and admire each other. Keep your sidekick close by for life!

7–11: POTENTIAL PRIMO PALS! She may be a best buddy in the making, but you'll have to iron out the quirks first! Right now you're not as compatible as best friends should be. Perhaps trust and respect just haven't been established yet. Keep working on the details and she may grow into a treasured friend.

0–6: OUCH! You two are muddling through whatever you do, and it's not working for either of you. Unless you sit down and talk, this union will be full of ups, downs, and hurt feelings. Try discussing the fundamentals of friendship like honesty, trust, openness, and acceptance. If you can come together, great! If you can't, there may be another best buddy for you!